All Sorts of Wa
in Liquorice Cou

Richard Bell
with recipes by
Barbara Bell

Contents

WILLOW
ISLAND
EDITIONS

In the Liquorice Fields

GLYCYRRHIZA GLABRA

'In the licorice fields at Pontefract
My love and I did meet'

wrote **John Betjeman** (using an old spelling of the plant's name) in 1954, but four years later only 5 acres of liquorice remained in Pontefract; on the site of the present hospital and Cobbler's Lane estate. The last commercial crop was harvested by Wilkinson's in 1968 so, on these walks, the only liquorice plant you're likely to see is in the herb garden below the castle keep *(left)* but there are plans to reintroduce the crop.

Betjeman *(1906-1984)* describes Pontefract's 'lowly streets where country stops, and little shuttered corner shops'.

Some of those corner shops have gone but, as in Betjeman's time, the country starts as soon as you step beyond the streets of Pontefract, Featherstone and Knottingley, as you'll discover on these walks.

Access

For the most part these walks follow public and permissive rights of way or cross public parks and open spaces but diversion orders can be made and permissions withdrawn. We cannot of course be held responsible for such diversion orders and any inaccuracies in the text which result from these or any other changes to the routes, nor for any damage which might result from walkers trespassing on private property. We'd be grateful if you would let us know about any changes to routes by e-mailing us: **richard@willowisland.co.uk**

Most of these walks can be muddy in places and, while checking them in early summer, we've discovered that it can be quite a struggle to cross a field of oilseed rape as harvest time approaches. There are a number of nettly paths too, so beware if you're wearing shorts!

Waterways and rivers: Several of the footpaths go close to open water. Always take special care of children when visiting waterways and towing paths, particularly near locks.

Maps: In case of blocked paths, it's always useful to have the appropriate OS Explorer map in your pocket to find an alternative route but, you've guessed it, Pontefract is right on the edge of three sheets: 289 Leeds, 278 Sheffield & Barnsley and 290 Selby.

Acknowledgements: My thanks to **Linda Banks** of Wakefield Tourist Information and **Heather Copley** of Copley's Farm Shop for suggesting Pontefract's liquorice as a subject and for all the advice, encouragement and information they've given me; to Wakefield Metropolitan District Council's **footpaths officers**, **David Holdsworth** and **Virginia Moulton**; to **Linda Ingham** for proofreading my text; to **Freya Sykes** of Ella Riley's Toffee Shop for suggesting the ice cream recipe and for supplying me with essential research material (all-sorts of liquorice confectionery!) and, finally, to our all-weather walks testers **Linda**, **Steve** and **Patch**.

A Brief History of Liquorice

August 1588: a Spanish galleon is wrecked off the Yorkshire coast as the defeated Armada heads north.

A Pontefract schoolmaster finds a bundle of sticks washed ashore.

While he uses the sticks to whack his pupils, they soon find the sticks are delicious . . . and that is how liquorice root - also known as Spanish - came to be planted in Pontefract.

But it's more likely that the monks of **St John's Priory** or the Friars of **Friarwood** (St Richard's) were the first to grow liquorice in Pontefract.

Liquorice contains **glycyrrhizin**, also known as glycyrrhizic acid, a sugar-like compound that is about 50 times sweeter than sucrose.

The scientific name of liquorice is *Glycyrrhiza glabra*. In Greek 'glykas' or 'glycor' means sweet and 'rhiza' means root.

But it's another sweet-tasting compound, **anetole**, also found in aniseed, fennel and star-anise *(below)* that gives liquorice its flavour.

Liquorice sticks were found in the tomb of Tutankhamen.

Soldiers in Alexander the Great's army chewed on liquorice to suppress thirst when they marched across the desert.

1863; liquorice was grown in the castle grounds which were rented out at £30 a year.

Liquorice has long been valued for its medicinal uses.

But like all medicines, too much can be bad for you!

Liquorice is used to flavour the Italian liqueur Sambuca and is also added to tobacco.

Chantry Chapel to Featherstone

THE NARROW three-arched bridge that you cross at the start of this walk is described as a **packhorse bridge**, probably dating from the 18th century. The parapets might be a later addition, as packhorse bridges were usually open at the sides to allow for overhanging baggage.

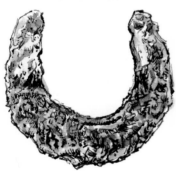

I found this **horse shoe** on the red shale path

between Warmfield Common and Mill Hill. It's about 13 cm (5 inches) across and encrusted with rust and mud. As the red shale is from a colliery spoil heap, I guess that it might be the shoe of a **pit pony**. In the 1930s the Featherstone Agricultural Show included a section for pit ponies.

A couple of ponies were tethered, grazing near the pond on **Warmfield Common**. Commons need some kind of grazing if they're going to remain as open spaces; if left they would gradually become woodland as birch and willow colonise open ground.

Reg Dunn, who lived in a flat in the stable block *(above)* at **Heath Hall**, remembered the Hall in its heyday. He told me that when there was a big party at the house the coachmen who had brought the guests there would get together in the room above the stables and have a gathering of their own, taking the guests home when the party ended.

Heath village

Chantry Chapel to Featherstone

7 miles, 11 km. 3 hours
Start from the **Chantry Chapel** Wakefield **O.S. ref**. SE 338 201

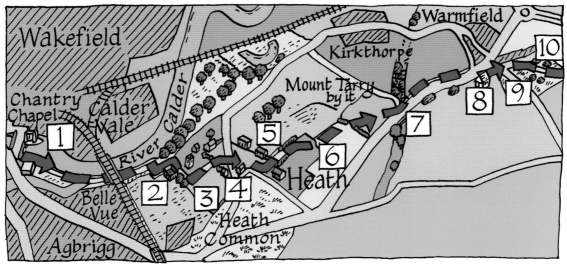

At the end of the walk, return by train from **Featherstone** to **Wakefield Kirkgate** or by buses 145, 148, 149 or 150 (or park at Featherstone and travel to Wakefield to start the walk).

1. With the chapel on your left, walk across the medieval **Wakefield Bridge** and turn immediately left over the packhorse bridge to follow the riverside path. In a quarter of a mile, cross the footbridge at **Fall Ings lock** and continue along the riverside path.

2. In another quarter of a mile the path turns away from the river; when you come out at the end of a concrete roadway turn left and then in 30 yards take the public footpath on your right after passing **Wakefield B electricity substation**.

3. After passing **Dame Mary Bolles water tower** on your left, turn left with the footpath up the hill.

4. An iron gate and a short track bring you out at **Heath** village; go straight ahead to the far side of the village green, crossing a road.

5. Turn right and after crossing two road/driveways you skirt around a **haha** (a combined low wall and ditch) in front of a house on your left then, when you reach a third roadway, turn left and look for a stile at the right-hand end of a high garden wall. Follow the footpath up the gentle slope of **Mount Tarry by it** (height 80 metres) on your left.

6. A kissing gate brings you out near the corner of a field. Cross the corner to find a second kissing gate then follow the path along the top side of the next field but as you reach the other end make your way towards a gap in the hedge, 70 yards from the top end of the hedge. Growing crops sometimes obscure the path across this corner.

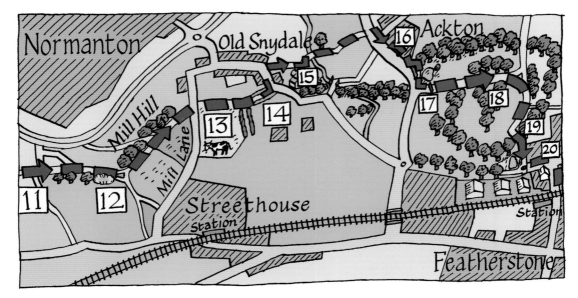

7. Cross the plank bridge into the next field then head diagonally across it to the bottom corner by the road. Turn left then climb **Pineapple Hill** alongside the busy A655.

8. Cross the road when you reach **The Pineapple public house** at the top of the hill, turn left then take the tarmac path across **Warmfield Common**.

9. Cross the road (**Crossley Street**) and continue in the same direction along **Elsicker Lane**.

10. Turn right on a stony track across the common, just before the lane bends to the left.

11. Continue on this track for half a mile, heading east, ignoring a footpath to the right and the left.

12. Pass a marshy area on your right then take the left-hand fork to climb the ridge of **Mill Hill** ahead. Turn left and follow the ridge-top path with the wood on your left.

13. Cross **Mill Lane** and continue on the footpath ahead along the left-hand side of a pasture.

14. A couple of stiles take you across the end of a farm track then along a grassy and in parts nettly path to **Old Snydale** village. When you come to the road opposite **Sunny Dairy Farm** turn left then in

200 yards, at **Crooklands Farm**, turn right down a lane.

15. In 200 yards, when the lane turns sharply to the left, take the footpath ahead along the right-hand edge of the field. Follow this footpath for half a mile, crossing a bridge over **Sewerbridge Beck** and passing through several metal kissing gates.

16. Cross the road and turn right, cross the end of **Ackton Lane** on your left then, in 100 yards, use the footpath set back from the road as you pass the houses of **Ackton village** on your left.
Cross **Ackton Crescent** then look for a metal kissing gate in the hedge on your left.

Go through it and turn right on the track for 200 yards.

17. Turn left, passing the car park of **Ackton Fishing Pool** on your left, then go through the gap at the side of the metal gate to follow the track ahead up the slope for half a mile.

18. At a Y-junction turn right then bear right on a track with a copse on your left. In 200 yards ignore a left-hand turn to **Featherstone**.

19. After crossing a railway sleeper bridge turn right with the path.

20. After passing a couple of ponds on your right, as the track curves to the right, take the rough path ahead into a corner by some warehouses. Turn left over a railway sleeper bridge onto **Green Lane**, then in 200 yards when you reach the **Featherstone Hotel**, turn right onto **Station Lane** and go to the platform at the far side of the level crossing to catch the train back to Wakefield Kirkgate. Alternatively you could extend this walk to Pontefract by continuing on the return half of the Halfpenny Lane walk.

The Murder of Longthorne

William Longthorne, aged 18, walked across Heath Common early on the morning of 17 October, 1828. He was on his way to try to find work at the stables at **Ferrybridge** which, being halfway between Edinburgh and London, was a busy stop for stage coaches.

He was accompanied by **William Mosey**, a 'low, broad-set, black-looking man', whom he'd met the day before in Wakefield. Witnesses said that Longthorne was dressed in a brown frock coat and drab cord breeches and carrying a bundle; and Mosey in a hairy cap, a blue-striped smock, and dirty cotton trousers.

At a little after 8 a.m., when they arrived near the footbridge across **Sewerbridge Beck** *(above, point 15 on the walk)* between Snydale and Ackton, Mosey attacked Longthorne, cut his throat with a razor, robbed him of 5 shillings and a small bundle of clothes, then dragged him by the feet and threw him into the beck. The cold water stopped the bleeding and Longthorne managed to crawl to the back door of **The Cross Keys**. A surgeon, Dr Buchanan from Loscoe, treated the wound but Longthorne died next morning. He is buried in Featherstone churchyard. Mosey was never caught and when he appeared back in the area 23 years later, Mr McDonnold, chief constable of Wakefield, decided that, because of the deaths of some of the witnesses, it was no longer possible to gather the evidence needed for a conviction.

Source: *Walks in Yorkshire: Wakefield, W. S. Banks, 1871*

Plaque on the footbridge.

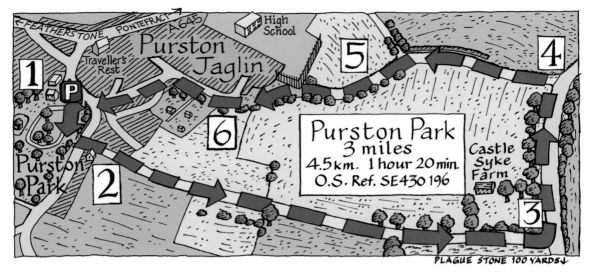

PLAGUE STONE 100 YARDS↓

Buses: 35, 146. Also, on the A645; 144, 145, 147, 149, 150, 157, 177.

Car park: if you're turning off the A645 into Purston on the B6421, the driveway is on your right after 100 yards on the corner of the junction with Ackworth Road.

1. Leaving the car park, with the park gates on your left, turn right in the direction of **Purston Hall** for a short distance then left at the circular bed to follow the tarmac perimeter path around the park in a clockwise direction. As soon as you get to the end of the rose garden on your

right, head off diagonally across the grassy slope towards the road.

2. Leave the park by a shallow gap in the banking and cross the road to take the public footpath signed

opposite which takes you on a farm track across the fields towards a low ridge.

3. After a mile, when you come out at a stone stile onto the **A628 Castle Syke Hill**, turn left on the pavement (turn right to see **The Plague Stone**).

4. As the road turns sharply to the right at the bottom of the hill, take the footpath on your left, a grassy track across the fields. There are deep ditches alongside the track.

5. After a third of a mile, ignore a footpath on your right and when you come out at the corner of the spiked fence around the school playing field bear left to continue with the hedgerow on your left.

6. You soon come out on **Little Lane**. Turn left and follow the lane for 300 yards then, at the give-way sign, turn left on **Wentbridge Road** to return to Purston Park. Turn right for the park gates when you reach the T-junction.

Purston Park

Purston working men's club, which stood near the Hall by the park gates was known as the 'Crow's Nest' because of a large rookery in the park.

Purston Lodge was built for local magistrate **Thomas Hall** *(c.1793-1857)* in the 1820s. It became **Purston Hall** in the 1860s when his son, the **Rev Thomas Hepworth Hall** *(1826-1871)* made substantial improvements, including installing Venetian blinds. In 1895 his son, **Percy Craven Hall** *(b.1859)*, let the Hall to **William Moore Wood**, the owner of Glasshoughton Colliery, then in 1925 he sold it for £2,750 to **Tommy Sides**, brewery owner, horse race organiser and sometime Mayor of Pontefract. Five years later Sides sold it to **Featherstone Urban Council** for £3,600. It served as the town hall for many years and was later an old folks' home before being sold for conversion into flats in 2007.

Purston Hall, built c.1824.

Heavyweight Champion

Champion bare-knuckle boxer **John Gully** *(1783-1863)* bought **Ackworth Park** in 1831 for £21,500 after winning £40,000 by betting on his own racehorse.

Gate lodge, Ackworth Park

Gully's last fight, against his great rival Bob Gregson, near Woburn on 10 May 1808 attracted a crowd of 20,000, prompting the authorities to call out the Dunstable Volunteers, as they feared that the French had invaded. Gully had retired from prize-fighting by the time he came to Ackworth but continued to make a fortune - and occasionally lose a fortune - out of horse racing. In 1832, the year he was elected as Member of Parliament for Pontefract, his horse, St Giles, won the Derby and he made a further £60,000.

Gully was twice married and had 12 children by each wife. His son, Robert, was shipwrecked on the island of Formosa (Taiwan) in 1842, where he was murdered by the Chinese.

Victorian graffiti

As you cross the **stone stile** *(point 3)* to Castle Syke Hill, look for this Victorian graffiti. September 11, 1891, was a Friday and September 17, 1901, was a Tuesday. Who were 'J *N* A' and 'C *N* P'? Perhaps we're looking for a "John 'n' Alice" and a "Charles 'n' Pauline". Queen Victoria died on the 22 of January 1901, so these two dates straddle the end of an era. Our 'John' could have served in the Boer War and 'Charles' in World War I.

*This **manhole cover** on Castle Syke Hill was cast at **The Model Foundry**, Ferrybridge, which employed 40 people and was founded in 1926 by **Samuel Gregg** (d.1950). It closed in 1968. One story has it that Gregg won the foundry and The Chestnuts, the house adjacent to it, in a poker game.*

The Plague Stone

*100 yards south of **Point 3**.* The Ackworth parish register for 1645 records that in the village that year 153 died of the plague. To prevent the spread of infection, the village cut itself off from the outside world. The hollow in the Plague Stone was filled with vinegar to disinfect the coins the villagers used to purchase supplies.

*Cast iron **milestone**, point 3.*

All Sorts of Landscapes

YOU CAN think of the bedrock beneath Pontefract as a rocky version of a liquorice all-sort - one of the sandwich variety - with white, brown and black layers.

Magnesian Limestone

This cream-coloured limestone was laid down 290 million years ago in a tropical sea. **Magnesian limestone** contains the mineral dolomite. It has been used for lime-burning, for crushed aggregate and as a building stone.

Magnesian limestone cutting, Leys Lane, Knottingley.

Basal Permian Sands

Earlier, near the edge of the sea, wind-blown desert sands formed dunes. These sands have been mined for glass-making and iron moulding.
Left: *limestone overlies the sands.*

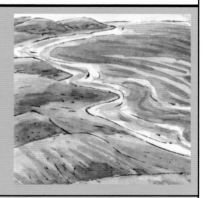

Coal Measures

300 million years ago: the peaty remains of tropical forests would become **coal**. **Sandstone** was laid down in river deltas, mudstone in calmer waters. **Mudstone** was used for brickmaking and **fireclay** for the manufacture of pottery, tiles and pipes.

Limestone Ridge

From East Hardwick *(point 9 on the next walk)* you can see the **ridge of magnesian limestone** to the east, lying on top of older rocks.

Pontefract Faults

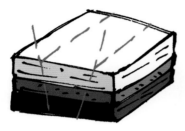

1. The uplift of the Pennines caused stresses in the rocks of Pontefract.

2. A block of rock slipped down between the North Pontefract Fault and the South Pontefract Fault.

3. So today - after erosion - you find limestone (under the town centre) alongside coal measures rocks.

Burning Well

In 1861, when a borehole near Featherstone station penetrated a layer of shale at a depth of 120 feet, at first water gushed up at the surface to a height of 30 feet. Later, as the pool at the surface bubbled 'like a witch's cauldron', the escaping gas, when lit with match, burned with a flickering red flame.

*Limestone lies on top of Basal Permian Sands at Mill Hill. Part of this **sand mine** was used as an air-raid shelter in World War II.*

Castle Syke Hill

I noticed **pebbles** scattered around the field at point 3 on the Purston Park walk. You'd normally find pebbles down in river valleys, so how did they get here? The geological map shows a patch of **till** (stony clay) on the hill top, dumped here by ice age glaciers perhaps 450,000 years ago.

High Ackworth

Part of the orignal inscription:
IMP CAES
MAR ANNIO FLORIANO

The foundation stone of the Early English Gothic style **St Stephen's**, East Hardwick *(above)*, was laid by Masonic Grand Master, the Marquess of Ripon, in 1872. The church was consecrated by the Archbishop of York in 1874.

TWICE A YEAR a sheaf of corn for the birds to feed on is hung from the staff of the statue of **St Cuthbert** in its niche over the porch of the church at High Ackworth. Appointed Bishop of Lindisfarne, Cuthbert *(c.635 - 687)*, was a hermit by inclination and liked to spend time amongst the sea-bird colonies on the Farne Islands. Eiders are still called 'Cuddy Ducks' in his honour.

This fragment of a **Roman milestone**, currently on display in Pontefract Museum, was found 300 yards north-west of Hundhill Farm, in 2002. It dates from the brief reign of **Emperor Florianus** *(232 - 276)* in the summer of 276 AD. He seized power on the death of his half-brother Emperor Tacitus in June, but in September, when civil war broke out, he was killed by his own men or possibly committed suicide.

Point 11: The Roman Road from Barnsdale Bar to Glasshoughton was improved under an Act of Parliament of 1819. It's now the modern A639.

Burnhill Bridge

River Went

Because of Viking raids, monks removed his body from Lindisfarne in 875. They may have paused at Ackworth on their travels around northern England. Cuthbert was reburied in Durham in 999.

Ermine Street, the Roman Road from Lincoln to York via Doncaster and Castleford, dates from *c.* 70 AD. The general Agricola and the emperors Hadrian and Septimius Severus must have travelled along it, as did **Constantine the Great** who was proclaimed emperor in York on 25 July 306 AD. Unlike Florianus, he defeated his rivals and became the first Roman emperor to convert to Christianity.

The **'Burial Field'** between High Ackworth and Hundhill *(point 4)* is said to be where the victims of the plague of 1645 were buried *(see page 10)*.

Village cross, High Ackworth
Left: *Look for this marker stone on the verge on your left after point 13, before you arrive at the Waste Water Treatment Works.*

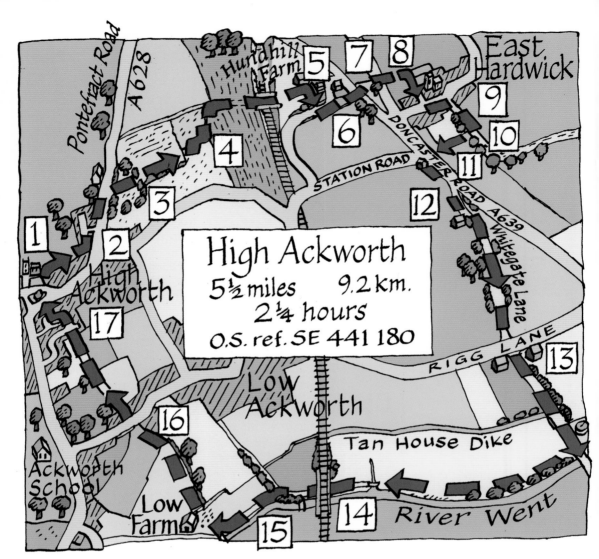

There is limited **parking** near **St Cuthbert's church** adjacent to the green triangle at the junction of the **A628 Pontefract Road** and the **B6421 Purston Lane**, **High Ackworth**.
Buses: 35, 47, 249.

1. From **Ackworth village cross**, take the footpath to the right of the **Manor House**, which stands immediately behind the cross. This takes you along the backs of

houses, then along the right-hand side of a field.

2. When the path emerges on the cul-de-sac of **Woodland Grove**, turn left then first right. When you get to the **Pontefract Road**, turn left for 150 yards, looking for a footpath sign in the hedgerow on your right.

3. Cross the road, take the three steps up the

roadside bank and then follow the footpath signed to the left across the field (occasionally blocked by a tall crop, in which case find your way around the field edge). After crossing a small plank bridge the path follows the right-hand side of the next field.

4. Keep going over a second plank bridge and

then at the third, the footpath turns left then right alongside the field boundary. When you reach a footpath coming in from the left, turn right across an open field towards the railway which is hidden in a cutting.

5. After crossing the railway, walk towards the high sandstone wall of **Hundhill Farm**, then turn right with the footpath. Turn left when you come out on **Hundhill Lane**.

6. As the lane turns to the left, take the stepped stile through the wall ahead.

7. In 200 yards another stone stile brings you out on **Sandy Gate Lane**; turn left then immediately right on a public footpath which takes you over a stile and along the left-hand side of a small field.

8. Cross the **A639** and continue ahead across the fields. You can see **East Hardwick church** to your right. When you arrive at a T-junction with another path, turn right towards the church (and perhaps take a break on the Hardwick Millennium seat).

9. Turn left through the village on **Darrington Lane** and in 150 yards take the public bridleway on your right between *Danes Lodge* and *Bridleways*.

10. In 250 yards take a footpath over the stile on your right, following the right-hand side of a pasture.

11. The stile directly ahead brings you out opposite the junction with **Station Road**; cross the **A639** and turn left following the grass verge alongside this busy stretch of road.

12. In 200 yards turn right on the public bridle-way along **Whitegate Lane**. In 150 yards the bridleway goes to the left of a driveway.

13. Cross **Rigg Lane** and continue on the track ahead. After passing **Ackworth Waste Water Treatment Works**, turn right on the footpath to 'Ackworth Moor Top, 1½ miles', with the small **River Went** to your left.

14. After three-quarters of a mile, you reach a railway viaduct; after going beneath it, ignore the first bridge over the

river on your left but in another 80 yards, in the corner of the field, take the public footpath to 'Ackworth Moor Top' on your left and cross the footbridge.

15. In 300 yards, when you arrive at a stone bridge across the river, turn right across a some-times muddy corner of the field to cross a stile by the metal gate, keeping the buildings of **Low Farm** on your left. Continue along the right-hand side of the next two fields until you come out via a stone stile on **Station Road**.

16. Cross the road to take the footpath between the houses diagonally opposite on your right. Follow this across the fields.

17. When you emerge on **Went Hill Close** make your way along **Hill Drive** ahead of you and in 150 yards take the cul-de-sac ahead. At the bottom left arm of the cul-de-sac take the footpath that runs behind the former **Mary Lowther Almshouses** *(1741)*, to emerge opposite **St Cuthbert's church**.

Pontefract Town Trail

L OCAL HISTORIAN **Harry Battye** *(1930–1979)* once grumbled that knocking buildings down was 'the traditional Pontefract answer to problems affecting architecture' but that wasn't always the case; sometimes they didn't knock them down – they blew them up! I'm not talking about the second civil war siege in June 1645, when the Roundheads pounded the tower of All Saints Church with 100 18lb cannonballs during a two day bombardment; much more recently, in the 1960s, **New Hall**, which dated from 1591, was dynamited by demolition experts from the National Coal Board who, in the process, blew out many windows on nearby Nevison estate!

But if you keep an eye out for blue plaques as you walk around Pontefract, and if you look up *above* the shop fronts in the market place, you'll realise that a large number of the town's historical buildings have survived.

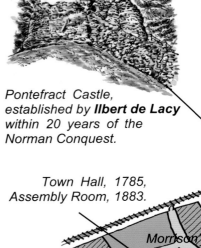

Pontefract Castle, established by **Ilbert de Lacy** within 20 years of the Norman Conquest.

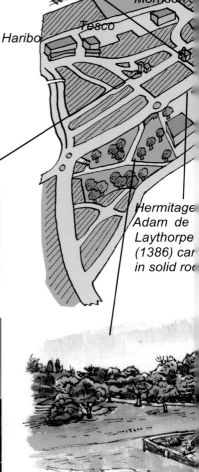

Town Hall, 1785, Assembly Room, 1883.

Morrison's

Tesco

Haribo

Hermitage Adam de Laythorpe (1386) car in solid roc

St Giles Church in the market place has been dubbed 'the crown of the town' but in 1792 local diarist John Byng dismissed the newly built tower as 'a hall of Grecian Fancies'. Under the later restorations there are still traces of its medieval walls. In 1177 Henry II gave Henry de Lacy, lord of the manor of Pontefract, the right to hold a fair on the feast of St Giles, 1 September.

Butter Cross, 1734.

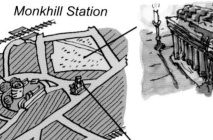

Monkhill Station

Baghill Station

ntefract General Infirmary

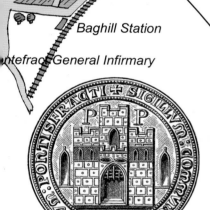

Pontefract Corporate Seal.

Valley Gardens; Friarwood valley was the site of St Richard's Friary est. 1256.

*The Church of **St John's Priory** (founded c.1090), stood to the left of the meadow in this panoramic photograph. In 1359 it is recorded that, to the right of the high altar, 'blood ran out of the tomb of Lord Thomas, formerly Earl of Lancaster at Pontefract.'*
*For the full story see my **Walks in Robin Hood's Yorkshire**.*

Pontefract's **Parish church of All Saints** is mentioned in the Domesday Book. In 1267 its vicar was **Antony Bek** *(c.1245-1311)* who rose to become Bishop of Durham *(1283)* and the chief investigator of the Knights Templar *(1308)*. He was given the title of Patriarch of Jerusalem by the Pope *(1306)*.

During the first civil war siege of Pontefract Castle, a group of 11 Royalist men and boys held the tower of the church for 5 days. They escaped to the castle by descending from the west end of the church using a bell rope, but their leader, **Captain Joshua Walker**, was wounded when the Roundheads opened fire on them.

In the autumn of 1536, during the northern uprising known as the Pilgrimage of Grace, the Archbishop of York was dragged from the pulpit by the rebels as he attempted to preach caution.

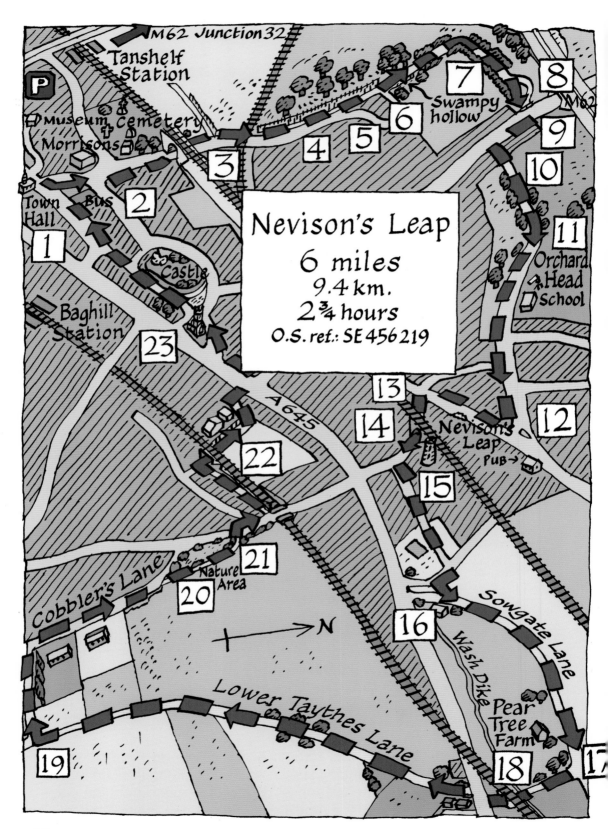

Nevison's Leap

6 miles
9.4 km.
2¾ hours
O.S. ref.: SE 456 219

Parking: town centre car parks. **Bus station**: nearby on **Horsefair**. Nearest **train stations**: **Tanshelf** and **Baghill**.

1. Starting from the **Market Place**, walk to the left side of the **Town Hall**, cross at the pedestrian crossing and turn left down **Finkle Street**. As soon as you've passed the back entrance to the bus station turn left and cross **Northgate** to walk down **Skinner Lane**, passing **Northgate Medical Centre** on your right and **Morrison's** across the road on your left.

2. Continue straight ahead down Skinner Lane, passing the cemetery on your left. A stone arch bridge takes you under the railway.

3. Ignore a footpath on your left and cross a second railway via the level crossing.

4. Continue with an estate of houses on your right and a banking of trees behind the spiked fence on your left.

5. Stay on the left all the way until **Lake View** turns to the right, then take the footpath ahead .

6. Ignore a footpath behind the houses on your right and continue ahead. Warning: in this wooded hollow the path can be swampy even in dry weather. Take care and use your own judgement; the alternatives are to wade through or double back a little to find a short but tricky unofficial diversion (not a public right of way) amongst the trees to the left. The path soon gets a lot better.

7. In a quarter of a mile bear right with the footpath which now follows a track heading in the direction of Ferrybridge cooling towers in the distance.

8. When the track swings to the left as you near the motorway, take the footpath down the slope ahead. You soon rejoin the track.

9. When you come out on **Spittal Hardwick Lane**, turn right, away from the motorway.

10. At the crest of the hill, turn left on the public footpath along **Orchard Head Lane** for quarter of a mile.

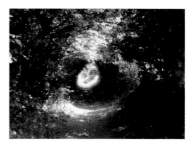

11. When you come out at a play area, continue on Orchard Head Lane ahead, passing **Orchard Head School** on your left.

12. In a third of a mile, at the T-junction with **Ferrybridge Road**, turn right downhill (or left to visit **Nevison's Leap** public house).

13. After passing **Nevison's Leap**, marked by a blue plaque on your left, turn next left at the foot of the hill on **Water Lane**.

14. After passing under the railway, look out for **Dandy Mill** on your left, then take the first turn left on **Dandy Mill Avenue**.

15. Ignoring **Highland Close** cul-de-sac on your left, continue on the avenue. Pass between concrete bollards onto **Stumpcross Meadows**, the continuation of the avenue. At the T-junction with **Stumpcross Lane** turn right.

16. In 50 yards turn left towards the fence of the **Waste Water Pumping Station** and turn left along a track, **Sowgate Lane**.

17. Just after passing **Pear Tree Farm** on your right, 100 yards before you reach the motorway, turn right on the footpath.

18. After passing under the railway, cross the **A645 Knottingley Road**, turn right and then almost immediately left, on a green lane, **Lower**

Taythes Lane, behind the row of houses.

19. After about three-quarters of a mile, turn right on the public bridleway, passing a row of nine Lombardy poplars.

20. Turn right and walk along **Cobblers Lane**, passing two schools on your right. As the lane turns to the left, take the green track ahead around **Cobblers Lane Nature Area**. There are views towards Pontefract across a low-lying area where liquorice was grown until the 1960s, while on a clear day you can see the North Yorks Moors on the horizon to the north, 36 miles away.

21. When the path brings you back down to the road, turn right (there's a brief view of one of Pontefract's two liquorice all-sorts factories, amongst the trees ahead to your left), but in 100 yards, just

before you reach the railway bridge, take the footpath on your left behind the backs of the houses, with the spiked fence of the railway on your right.

22. In 300 yards, turn right through an underpass beneath the railway and follow the path (**Atkinson Lane**) behind an industrial estate and across a footbridge until you come out on the **A645**.

Cross the road and turn left then take the first right after the filling station on **North Baileygate** passing the church on your left.

23. Cross the road and walk up **Castle Garth** ahead. Pass the castle on your right and continue straight ahead down **Micklegate** to return via **Horsefair** to the town hall.

'Swift Nick'

HIGHWAYMAN 'Swift Nick' **John Nevison's** *(1639-1684)* dawn to dusk ride from Gad's Hill, Kent, to York was later attributed to Dick Turpin. A blue plaque *(point 12 on this walk)* marks the

spot where he made his leap on horseback across what was then a narrow gorge. He was eventually arrested at **The Three Houses Inn**

at Sandal, Wakefield, and subsequently hanged in York.

Military Depot

The Old Military Depot *(bottom, right)*, Back Northgate, was built for the Pontefract Corps of the **West Yorkshire Rifle Volunteers**, formed in 1859. They built shooting butts in the park and drilled with such enthusiasm that a wall alongside their parade ground collapsed, falling onto the railings of the adjacent cemetery. The Old Military Depot became **King Edward's Grammar School** on May Day 1890.

The town became the garrison of the **7th Brigade** (55th and 84th Regiments of Foot) which occupied the **Baghill Barracks** from 1878. The Barracks closed in 1963. On the

Halfpenny Lane walk, point 12, you pass a **marker stone** that I guess is a associated with the Barracks.

Dandy Mill erected as the 'Boreas Union Mill' in 1819. The brickwork was tarred to make it weatherproof.

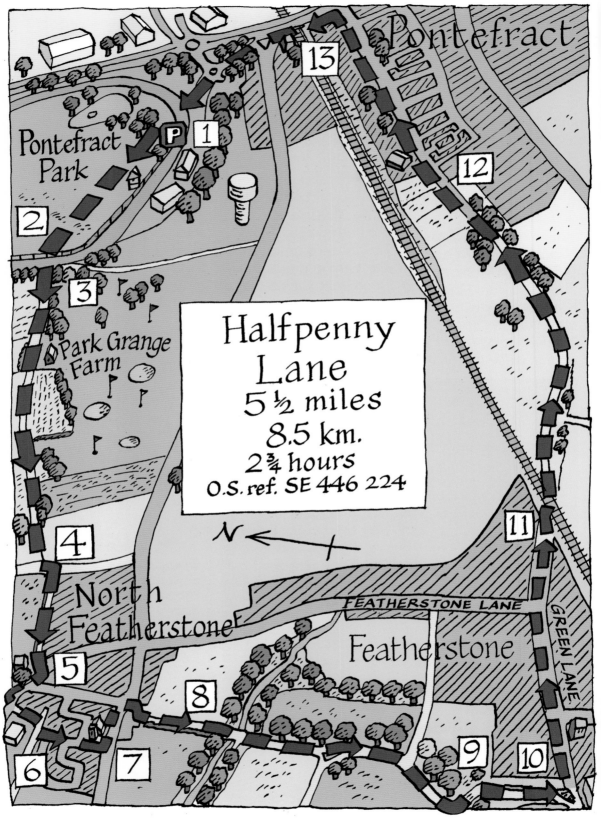

Pontefract

Pontefract
Park

P

1

13

12

2

3

Park Grange
Farm

Halfpenny
Lane
5½ miles
8.5 km.
2¾ hours
O.S. ref. SE 446 224

N

4

11

North
Featherstone

FEATHERSTONE LANE

Featherstone

GREEN LANE

5

8

6

7

9

10

Car park: Pontefract Park; you cross the racetrack to reach this after taking the fourth exit from the roundabout as you approach from Pontefract.

1. Find the footpath between the car park and park then, with the path behind you, set out across the open grassy area keeping the grandstand and stewards' look-out post to your left and playing fields to your right. This footpath isn't waymarked but you pick up its line again when you cross a rough grassy area.

2. A little to the right of the 3 furlong marker, look for the footpath sign in the hedgerow at the far side of the racetrack. The right of way across the track isn't marked; you have to duck under the railings immediately to the right of where the wire fence ends between the corner on your left and the straight stretch on your right.

3. Cross the track to follow the footpath marked 'North Featherstone, 1 mile'. Pass **Park Grange Farm** on your left and continue on the path straight across the fields ahead. You're heading for the right-hand edge of **North Featherstone** on the ridge.

4. When you reach the farm track go through the metal kissing gate and turn left and then immediately right on a footpath marked 'Willow Lane, ¼ mile'. This goes behind houses along the edge of a field.

5. Turn right, passing **The Bradley Arms** on your right and just before you reach the driveway to **St Wilfrid's Catholic High School** on your left, turn left on the public footpath.

6. At the end of the school fence turn right then immediately left on a path that soon brings you out on a small street.

7. Walk down the street ahead, turn left around **All Saints churchyard** then in 150 yards, at the bend, turn right and cross Church Lane. Pass **Almond Cottage** and the driveway to **11B** on your right, then find the footpath down the right side of the next driveway.

8. Follow the footpath with a hawthorn hedge on your right down to a crossroads of tracks, then go straight ahead up the slope and at the top continue ahead, ignoring a track on your right at a Y-junction and later a track on your left to Featherstone.

9. After crossing a railway sleeper bridge turn right with the path.

10. After passing a couple of ponds on your right, as the track curves to the right, take the rough path ahead into a corner by some warehouses. Turn left over a railway sleeper bridge and continue straight ahead for half a mile along the entire length of **Green Lane**, which finally becomes a cycle track (turn right to the station at **The Featherstone Hotel** if you'd like break your journey here and return to Pontefract on the train).

11. When you come to the railway, cross it with care and continue on the cycleway with the railway on your left.

12. When you reach the end of the cycleway continue along **Halfpenny Lane** ahead, passing the **Prince of Wales Hospice** on your left.

13. At the end of Halfpenny Lane, turn left at the T-junction and walk alongside the dual-carriageway for 300 yards then, after crossing the railway bridge, cross the pedestrian crossing and take the tree-lined avenue ahead to return to the car park.

All Saints' Church, Featherstone

A Roundhead and a Royalist are buried in Featherstone church; **Langdale Sunderland** *(1618-1698)* of Ackton Hall was captain of a troop of horse and fought for the king at Marston Moor. He was fined £878 by Cromwell. One of the 3 bells of the church bears his initials and the date 1682. Lying nearby is **Nicolas Fairfax** *(d. 1657)*, who fought for the Parliamentarians.

Murder victim **William Longthorne** *(see page 7)* is buried to the east of the church but I wasn't able to find his headstone.

The Featherstone Massacre

The home secretary, Morley-born **Herbert Asquith** *(1852-1926)*, was dubbed 'Featherstone Asquith' or the 'Featherstone Murderer' for his mishandling of the tragic events which took place on 7 September 1893, when troops opened fire on a crowd of 'locked-out' miners and onlookers. Two men were killed. The confrontation took place at Ackton Hall Colliery on **Green Lane**, then known as Featherstone Common Lane.

Night Flight

At **Pontefract Gala** in July 1864, at 9.30 p.m., a balloon, filled at the gasworks, was launched from fields to the south of Half-penny Lane.

'Mrs Metcalfe, wife of the proprietor of the balloon, was seated in the car, and waved her handkerchief as the ascent commenced.' The *Pontefract Advertiser* reports that the balloon sailed off across the town and descended half an hour later, 8 miles to the west at Haddlesey near Eggborough.

The hedgerow (in the distance in this drawing) that comes down to Halfpenny Lane from the southern boundary of the Crematorium marks the course of Roman Ermine Street.

Plaque on the gable end of a house on the corner of Lime Tree Avenue and Halfpenny Lane.

Racing started in Pontefract in 1720. A brick-built grandstand was added in 1802 but it was demolished by irate townsfolk in 1844 when the track closed, and they stood to lose their investment. A new stand was built in 1879.

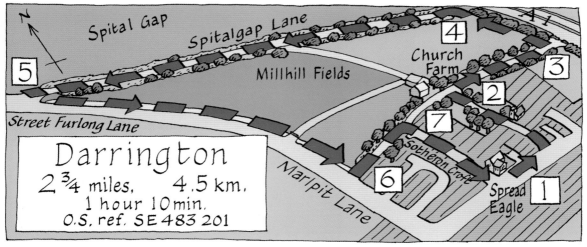

Street Furlong Lane

Darrington
2 ¾ miles.   4.5 km.
1 hour 10 min.
O.S. ref. SE 483 201

Parking: there are a few spaces on **Estcourt Road**, opposite **The Spread Eagle** public house.

1. With The Spread Eagle on your left walk along Estcourt Road to the post office then turn left on **Philips Lane**.

Darrington Jubilee Church House, 1887.

2. Walk past the church and church house, and at the top end of the lane, turn right on a public footpath.

3. Just before you get to the A1, turn left alongside the edge of the field.

4. When you come out on **Spitalgap Lane**, turn left.

5. At the end of the lane, turn left to return towards the village.

6. As you reach the village, turn left on the public footpath alongside houses on your right.

7. In 250 yards, turn right down the first road you come to, **Sotheron Croft**, to return to The Spread Eagle at the start of this walk.

St Luke's has a much-rebuilt tower that might date from Saxon times and, if you look in at the porch, a 13th century arch around the door. **Sir Warin de Scragil**, who fought in the Battle of Bannockburn, 1314, is buried near the altar. His effigy depicts him wearing chain-mail.

J. S. Fletcher *(1863-1935)* wrote *Memorials of a Yorkshire Parish - An Historical Sketch of the Parish of Darrington (1915)* and his novel *When Charles I was King* is set in Darrington, while *The Town of Crooked Ways*, is based on Pontefract.

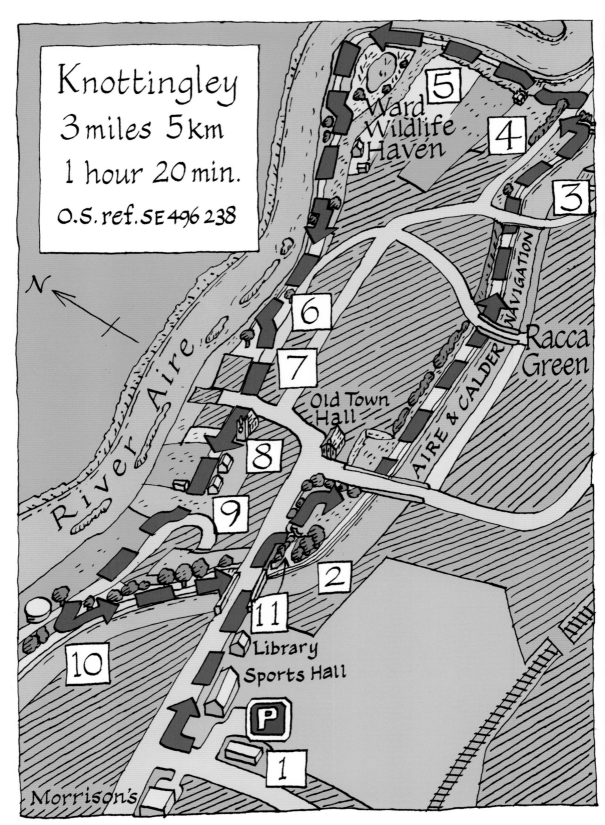

Knottingley
3 miles 5km
1 hour 20 min.
O.S. ref. SE 496 238

N

River Aire

Ward
Wildlife
Haven

5

4

3

6

7

Old Town
Hall

Racca
Green

AIRE & CALDER NAVIGATION

8

9

2

11

10

Library
Sports Hall

P

1

Morrison's

Knottingley

Car park: behind the sports centre (entrance opposite the entrance to Morrisons' car park). The towpath is not a public right of way but British Waterways encourage responsible leisure use of the towpath. Please take special care of children on this waterside walk.

1. Walk back up to the main road and turn right. After passing the library and crossing the bridge over the canal, take the path through the gap in the wall to the top of a small terraced amphitheatre.

2. Turn left, following the path down the slope and continue around the grassy area turning left on the towpath under **Jackson's Bridge**. Continue on the towpath under the **Cow Lane** and **Shepherd's Bridges**.

3. When you reach **Trundle's Lane Bridge**, walk up the 3 railway sleeper steps, turn left on the track and then right at the T-junction with the next track.

4. In 100 yards turn left onto the playing fields via a metal barrier and, following the foot of the riverside banking on your right, walk towards the electricity substation in the corner. Take the grassy path up to the embankment-top footpath and turn left to follow it for three-quarters of a mile, with the river on your right.

5. Go through a kissing gate and turn right to continue on the riverside path around **Ward Wildlife Haven** (in times of flooding turn left along the embankment to point 6).

6. When you leave the Wildlife Haven via the kissing gate, continue with the concrete flood wall on your right. You emerge at the end of a track; turn right with the flats on your left.

7. After following the flood wall alongside a small strip of riverside parkland, bear left with the path and then follow the road towards the church ahead.

8. Continue with the church on your left, passing Manor Barn on your left.

9. Follow the path across a paddock and, when you come out on the bend of a road, bear right to follow the road ahead.

10. Just before you reach the gates of **King's Mill**, take the path on your left down to the canal then turn left along the towpath.

11. After passing under **Gagg's Bridge** look for a woodland path that takes you back to the amphitheatre and climb the steps to return to the road. Turn left to return to the car park.

Knottingley

AT HARKER'S shipyard they've built coal barges, trawlers, coasters, cod liver oil barges, World War II landing craft, tugs, passenger launches, an ice breaker (for British Waterways) and dumb barges, better known as 'Tom Puddings', which were towed along the canal by a barge in the way an engine would pull a series of coal trucks. The first vessel built at Harker's was the 95ft, 150 ton coastal tanker *William*

Kipping, which was launched on the 18 November 1929.

In the days of sail, shipbuilders such as Garlick, Cliffe and Worfolk of Knottingley built sloops (1 mast), ketches (2 masts) and schooners (2-4 masts). It's thought that troop transports for the Crimean War were built in a shipyard not far from Jackson's Bridge.

Keels, shallow-hulled timber vessels resembling

Viking longships, were used in medieval times to take cargoes of wool down river from Knottingley. Traditional single-mast, square-sailed keels were still sailing the local waterways in the 1890s.

The Aire and Calder Navigation Act of 1699 was passed to improve navigation along the rivers. **The Knottingley Canal** was opened at 10 a.m. on 20 July 1826.

On the canal side of the town hall there was a **ropewalk** – a street where long strands of hemp were laid out, ready for twisting into rope.

In his *Home Tour*, **George Head** describes how, in 1834, you could travel in style from Goole to Knottingley on **The Twin Boat**, a gaudily decorated 'floating house' with seven windows on each side and 'a gigantic portrait of Queen

Manor Farm, the oldest domestic building in Knottingley, is said to be the place where the last bull-baiting in England was held before the so-called sport was banned in 1823.

Adelaide on her quarter'. It was towed by four 'nearly thoroughbred' horses, three of them ridden by small boys in blue, red and white uniform. With a change of horses mid-way, the journey was completed in a little over 2 hours. A year later the Twin Boat was no longer in operation and Head complained that the same journey took him

Knottingley Town Hall

theatre or, later, a cinema. The basement housed a swimming baths.

Cutting through the limestone by the M62

twice as long by paddle-steamer as one of the paddles broke before they left the dock in Goole.

1837 the steam packet the *Magnet* departed for Goole at 6.30 a.m. daily.

Town Hall

The **Town Hall** was built in 1865 thanks to the efforts of a group of townspeople who included a pottery manufacturer, a lime merchant, two shipbuilders and a rope maker. It had a library, a newsroom and a public room which could serve as a dance hall,

Glass manufacture in the area goes back to Roman times; **Lagentium** - the Roman name for Castleford - means 'the place of the bottle-makers'.

In 1866 Ferrybridge postmaster **Joshua Arnall** invented the

St Botolph's Church tower was built in 1873.

first semi-automatic **bottle-making machine**.

The **Knottingley Brewery** produced porter, a dark-brown bitter beer flavoured with liquorice.

In 1861 Knottingley had 13 firms producing **limestone** for agriculture and road building. As you can see at Jackson's Bridge, it was excavated to a depth of 7 yards but below that the quarry-men hit the water table.

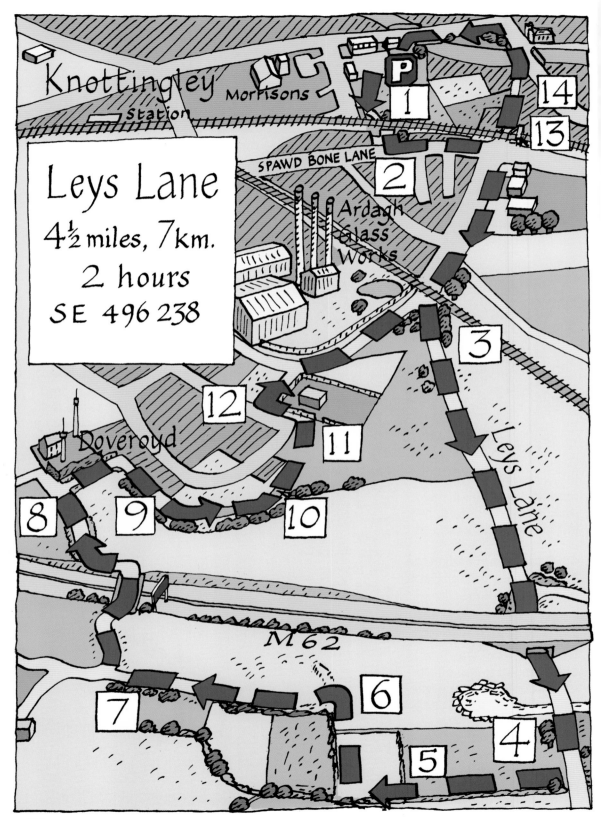

Leys Lane
4½ miles, 7km.
2 hours
SE 496 238

Knottingley
station
Morrisons
P
1
14
13
SPAWD BONE LANE
2
Ardagh Glass Works
3
Leys Lane
12
Doveroyd
11
8
9
10
M 62
7
6
5
4

Car park: as previous walk.

1. With your back to the swimming pool, cross the car park, passing **Kellingley Welfare Football Club** ground on your left to join the footpath which takes you under the railway.

2. When you reach **Spawd Bone Lane** turn left and continue for 300 yards then, when you reach the level crossing and footbridge on your left, turn right on **England Lane**. After passing **The White Swan**, **Ash Grove Medical Centre** and **England Lane School** on your left you reach the end of the lane; take the public footpath straight ahead.

3. After crossing the railway, take the left-hand path ahead for half a mile.

4. After taking the underpass beneath the M62, you cross a quarry service road (in regular use when we checked out this walk) then in 150 yards, when you reach the far side of the next field, turn right on an indistinct footpath with the field boundary on your left and follow it for a quarter of a mile.

5. You'll notice that the next field boundary that you pass on your right lines up with the three chimneys of the glassworks. Ignore this but in 100 yards turn right at the next field boundary, heading a little to the left of the three chimneys, keeping the field boundary on your left.

6. In 250 yards turn left at the end of this field (don't continue towards the trees alongside the motorway) and you soon find yourself on a more definite farm track ahead.

7. At the T-junction with the bend of a farm track, turn right. Cross the bridge over the M62 and continue with the track.

8. At the end of the field, before you reach **Dove-royd House**, turn right on the footpath in front of the hedge towards the housing estate.

9. Go through the squeeze stile and turn right to follow the path around the perimeter of the estate, keeping the hawthorn hedge on your right.

10. When you come to the playing fields, walk along the left side in the direction of the three chimneys in the distance.

11. Leaving the playing fields via the gate, turn right on **Windermere Drive**, then turn left with the road.

12. Opposite **Throstle Row**, turn right on the public bridleway then at the T-junction with a footpath, turn right to return to the level crossing at point 3 of this walk.

13. Return along **England Lane** and take the footbridge or – with great care – the level crossing ahead.

14. Take the footpath ahead next to the gates of **Knottingley Town Cricket Club**. In 100 yards, ignoring an entrance to the playing fields on your left continue on the footpath ahead and you come out by the bridge over the canal. Turn left over the bridge (there's no pavement, so you might prefer to cross the road) to return along the A645 to the start of this walk. You can take a short cut to the car park via the grounds of the library.

Pontefract Cake Ice Cream

Take this ice cream out of the freezer an hour before serving and let it thaw slowly in the fridge.

Chop the Pontefract cakes into small dice and put into a heavy-based saucepan with the sugar, milk and vanilla essence.

In a bowl, lightly whisk the egg yolks and, in a separate bowl, lightly whip the cream. Set these to one side.

85g sugar
150ml skimmed milk
4 large egg yolks
570ml double cream
1 teaspoon vanilla essence
85g Pontefract cakes

Put the pan on a gentle heat and stir until the sugar is dissolved, then boil for three minutes. Use a timer.

Remove from the heat and cool for one minute, again using a kitchen timer, then stir in the whisked egg yolks and carefully fold in the cream.

Pour the mixture into a 1.5 litre freezable container with a lid.

Leave in the freezer for about 2 hours until the mixture is just beginning to freeze around the edges, then remove from the freezer and give it a good stir, mixing the outside to the more liquid middle. Return to the freezer for a further 2 hours and stir again; this prevents large ice crystals forming

Return to the freezer until solid.

Liquorice Langue du Chat

Here's a use for those leftover egg whites; these crisp biscuits with a hint of liquorice go well with ice cream.

Mix the sugar, almonds, flour and liquorice powder together in a bowl.

In a separate bowl, whip the egg whites until firm.

4 egg whites
110g caster sugar
110g ground almonds
2 level teaspoons liquorice powder*
2 heaped teaspoons plain flour

makes about 35 biscuits

Our thanks to Copley's Farm Shop for helping us track down this ingredient.

Carefully fold the dry ingredients into the egg whites.

Put the mixture into a piping bag and pipe fingers about 8 cm long onto baking sheets lined with baking parchment.

Bake in a pre-heated oven at 140°C for 30 minutes, then turn off the oven and leave in the oven until cold.